MY PALS ARE HERE!

Science

Energy

2nd Edition

Primary 3&4

Activity Book

Teo-Gwan Wai Lan
Science Education Consultant: Dr Charles Chew

Marshall Cavendish
Education

Preface

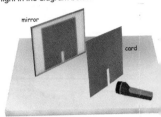

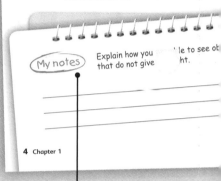

MY PALS ARE HERE! Science Activity Book provides a stimulating, hands-on approach to the learning of Science. Complementing the Textbook, it sets the context for pupils to experience first-hand the process of seeking answers to questions in an exciting and interesting way.

The activities in this book are presented in a variety of formats. There are experiments and investigations, projects and even activities that encourage outdoor exploration.

My notes
Provides opportunities for pupils to reflect and communicate what they have learnt

Process skills
Are highlighted to help pupils and teachers identify the process skills to be learnt in an activity

Name: _____ Class: _____ Date: _____

Activity 1.3 Measuring the brightness of light

Hands ON

Process skills: Observing • Inferring

We can see through some materials but not others. Why? Carry out this activity to find out!

Aim: To observe and measure the brightness of light passing through some materials

Materials needed: Three different materials (given by your teacher), torch, light sensor, datalogger

light sensor

torch

datalogger

(A datalogger, connected to a sensor, is used for measuring, recording and displaying data on a computer when you conduct an experiment. There are many types of dataloggers.)

Procedure to carry out

In this activity, you will learn how to use a datalogger.

(Handle the datalogger and sensor with care. Store them properly after

Light and sl

Hands ON
Comprises experiments and investigations to help pupils explore the scientific concepts

Process recess
Introduces skills essential for carrying out scientific inquiry and practical work to pupils

Name: _____ Class: _____ Date: _____

Process recess

The things that you can change in an experiment are called variables or factors. For a fair test, only one variable can be changed to show how it affects the results of the experiment. The rest of the variables have to be kept the same.

6. (a) Find out if the experiment was a fair test by completing the table below.

Variables of the experiment	Same	Different
Size of eggs		
Temperature of the water in the two beakers at the beginning of the experiment		
Amount of water the eggs were placed in		
Length of time the eggs were placed in the water		

(b) Look at the table above. Was the experiment a fair test?

_____

Activity
Engages pupils and develops their process skills

Name: _____ Class: _____ Date: _____

Activity 3.6 Keep it hot

Project

s: Using apparatus • Inferring • Planning

Aim: To plan an experiment to find out which type of cup is best for keeping a drink warm

Materials needed: Styrofoam, metal and ceramic cups, thermometer, measuring cylinder, watch, basin of tap water, hot water (about 70 °C)

You may use the experiment planner that is provided below to plan your experiment.

ceramic cup

styrofoam cup

metal cup

Procedure to carry out

1. Pour the same amount of hot water into all three cups.
2. Use a thermometer to measure the temperature of the water in all the cups.
3. Record your results in the table on the next page.
4. Place all the cups in a basin of tap water.
5. After three minutes, measure the temperature of the water in the cups again and write it down in the table provided on the next page.

Experiment Planner

Variable to change: _____

Project
Extended activity that involves research and data collection, helping pupils acquaint themselves with carrying out a complete experiment or investigation and presenting their findings

Contents

Energy

Activity 1.1 The shoebox experiment

Aim: To show that an object can be seen when there is light

Materials needed: Pencil case, two shoeboxes, torch

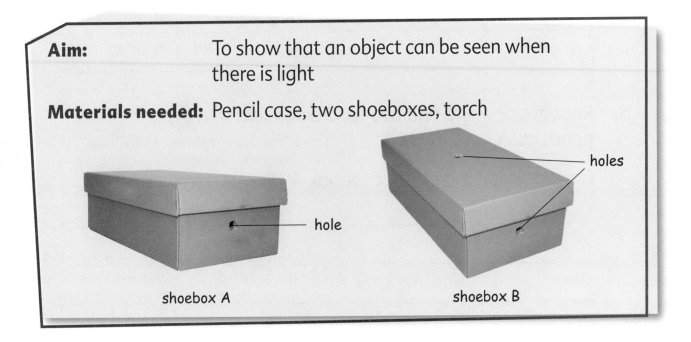

shoebox A

shoebox B

hole

holes

Procedure to carry out

1. Place the pencil case in shoebox A.

2. Peep through the hole on the side of shoebox A.

    Can you see the pencil case? Explain why.

    _____

    _____

    _____

3. Place the pencil case in shoebox B.

4. Peep through the hole on the side of shoebox B.

   Can you see the pencil case? Explain why.

   _____

   _____

   _____

5. Repeat steps one and two. Use a lighted torch instead of a pencil case.

   Can you see the torch in shoebox A? Explain why.

   _____

   _____

   _____

Conclusion

Objects can be seen when they _____ light or when they

give off their own _____.

My notes Do you know why you are still able to see at night when the sky turns dark?

   _____

   _____

   _____

Name: _____ Class: _____ Date: _____

Activity 1.2 A path of light

Aim: To observe how light travels

Materials needed: Torch, card with a narrow slit, mirror

Procedure to carry out

1. Place the torch and card on a table as shown.

2. Switch off all the lights in the room.

3. Switch on the torch and shine at side B of the card.

4. Observe where the light falls on side A of the card.

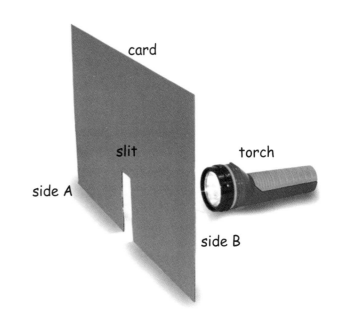

5. (a) Draw what you observe in the diagram shown above.

    (b) What have you learnt from this experiment? Circle the correct word in each bracket.

    Light (can/cannot) pass through the card. Light from the torch (can/cannot) pass through the slit. A beam of light is (formed/blocked) when light passes through the slit.

6. (a) Place a mirror in front of the beam of light that goes through the slit. Draw what happens to the beam of light in the diagram below.

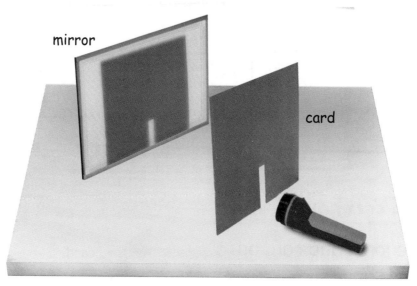

(b) What have you learnt from this experiment? Circle the correct word in each bracket.

The direction of the path of the beam of light (changes/does not change) when it falls on the mirror. This is because the mirror (reflects/does not reflect) light.

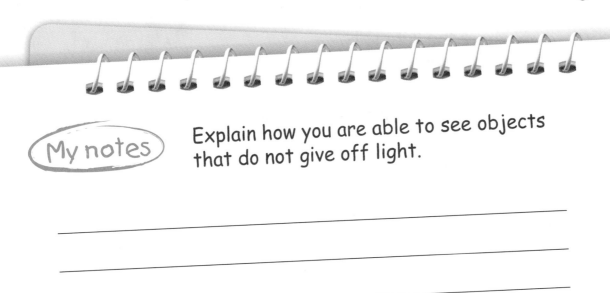

My notes

Explain how you are able to see objects that do not give off light.

_____

_____

_____

_____

Activity 1.3 Measuring the brightness of light

We can see through some materials but not others. Why?
Carry out this activity to find out!

Aim: To observe and measure the brightness of light passing through some materials

Materials needed: Three different materials (given by your teacher), torch, light sensor, datalogger

torch

light sensor

datalogger

(A datalogger, connected to a sensor, is used for measuring, recording and displaying data on a computer when you conduct an experiment. There are many types of dataloggers.)

Procedure to carry out

In this activity, you will learn how to use a datalogger.

(Handle the datalogger and sensor with care. Store them properly after use.)

1. Place the three materials in front of a torch, one at a time.

2. Attach the light sensor to the datalogger. Use it to measure the brightness of light passing through each material.

    (Note: Always remember to place the sensor at the same distance away from the torch for every test.)

Material	How clearly can you see the light through these materials?	Light sensor reading	Do you know why?

Results of an experiment can be shown in a graph. Let's learn how to read a graph.

3. An experiment was carried out. A torch was placed at different distances from the light sensor connected to a datalogger. Look at the graph that was produced by the datalogger. The level of brightness of light is measured in **lux**.

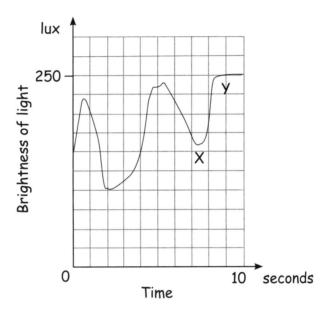

(a) Use a red pen to draw over the vertical axis and a blue pen to draw over the horizontal axis.

When the level of brightness measured by the light sensor is higher, the graph will move up. You can find out how bright the light is by reading the number along the vertical axis.

(b) What is the brightest level of light recorded in the graph?

The brightest level of light recorded in the graph is

_____ lux.

(c) Was the torch moving further or closer to the light sensor from point X to Y of the graph?

The torch was moving _____ to the light sensor.

Activity 1.4 Big and small shadows

Aim: To observe how a shadow changes when an object is moved closer to the light source

Materials needed: Sticky tape, white paper, torch, 1-metre ruler, styrofoam cup, pencil

Procedure to carry out

1. Paste a piece of white paper on the wall.

2. Place a ruler on the table with the zero-mark end against the paper.

3. Draw a short line on the side of the styrofoam cup. Use this mark to position the cup against the 5 cm mark on the ruler.

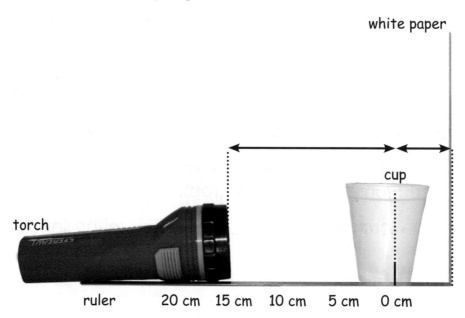

4. Switch on the torch and place it 15 cm away from the cup.

5. Trace the shadow on the white paper and label the shadow A.

6. Place the torch 10 cm away from the cup, trace the shadow and label it B.

7. Place the torch 5 cm away from the cup, trace the shadow and label it C.

   (a) Measure the height of the shadows from the tracings. Record the measurements in the table below.

Shadow	Distance between the cup and torch (cm)	Height of shadow (cm)
A	15	
B	10	
C	5	

   (b) (i) How do you make a bigger shadow of the cup?

   _____

   _____

   _____

   (ii) How do you make a smaller shadow of the cup?

   _____

   _____

   _____

BLANK

Name: _____ Class: _____ Date: _____

Activity 2.1 Hotter or colder

Process skills: Observing • Inferring

Aim: To test how well my skin can sense whether something is hot or cold

Materials needed: A basin of ice water, towel

⟨ **Procedure to carry out** ⟩

1. Put your right hand in a basin of ice water for ten seconds.

2. Remove your hand from the basin and dry your hand with a towel.

3. Then, place both your hands on your forehead at the same time.

ice water

(a) (i) Does your forehead feel the same to both your hands?

_____

(ii) To which hand does your forehead feel hotter?

_____

(iii) To which hand does your forehead feel normal?

_____

4. Now place your left hand in the ice water for ten seconds. Remove your hand from the basin and dry your hand. Then touch your forehead with both hands.

Write down your observation.

_____

_____

ice water

Conclusion

The hand placed in the ice water becomes _____ than the other hand. When both hands are placed on the forehead, the forehead feels _____ to the _____ hand.

My notes   How well can you trust your sense of touch to find out if you have a fever?

_____

_____

_____

_____

Activity 2.2 Raising temperature

Aim:	To measure temperature accurately
Materials needed:	Laboratory thermometer, equal amounts of warm and ice water, plastic spoon

Procedure to carry out

1. Examine a laboratory thermometer closely.

2. Look at the markings on your thermometer.

   (a) The smallest number is _____.

   (b) The largest number is _____.

   (c) The unit of measurement is _____.

   (d) The symbol is _____.

3. Place the thermometer in some warm water. Observe the liquid level in the thermometer.

   (a) What happened to the liquid level?

   _____.

Read the temperature after the liquid level stops changing.

(b) What is the temperature of the warm water?

_____

(Note: Always rinse the thermometer with running tap water and wipe it dry before taking the next measurement.)

4. Place the thermometer in ice water. Observe the liquid level in the thermometer.

(a) What happened to the liquid level?

_____

(b) What is the temperature of the ice water?

_____

5. Predict what the temperature will be if you mix the warm and ice water.

(a) Your prediction: _____

Pour the cold water into the warm water quickly. Stir the water a few times with the plastic spoon. Measure and record the temperature.

(b) The actual temperature: _____

Conclusion

Something that is hot has a _____ temperature than something that is cold.

Activity 2.3 Let's 'eggsperiment'

Process skills: Observing • Comparing • Concluding

Aim:	To find out the difference between heat and temperature
Materials needed:	1ℓ of hot boiling water, laboratory thermometer, two eggs, two plastic cups, two beakers

Procedure to carry out

Your teacher will carry out this experiment.

1. Boil the water. Once the water boils, measure its temperature.

   The temperature of the water is _____ °C.

2. Crack an egg into each plastic cup.

3. Pour 250 ml of hot water into one beaker and 750 ml of hot water into the other beaker.

250 ml

750 ml

4. Pour the eggs, one into each beaker of hot water, at the same time.

5. Compare the eggs after three minutes. Describe what you see.

    (a) Egg in the beaker with 250 ml of hot water:

    _____

    (b) Egg in the beaker with 750 ml of hot water:

    _____

Conclusion

The water in the two beakers has the same _____.

However, there is more hot water in one beaker than the other.

Therefore, the egg in the beaker containing 750 ml of hot water

was _____ cooked than the one in the beaker

containing 250 ml of hot water.

Since heat is needed to cook the eggs, the 750 ml of hot water

must have _____ heat than the 250 ml of hot water.

The things that you can change in an experiment are called variables or factors. For a fair test, only one variable can be changed to show how it affects the results of the experiment. The rest of the variables have to be kept the same.

6. (a) Find out if the experiment was a fair test by completing the table below.

Variables of the experiment	Same	Different
Size of eggs		
Temperature of the water in the two beakers at the beginning of the experiment		
Amount of water the eggs were placed in		
Length of time the eggs were placed in the water		

(b) Look at the table above. Was the experiment a fair test?

_____

Activity 2.4 Heat flows

Aim: To show that heat flows from hot to cold things

Materials needed: Basin, beaker, same amount of hot water and cold water, datalogger with heat sensor or a thermometer, two similar metal spoons, two cups

Procedure to carry out

Temperature is a measurement of how hot or cold an object is. You will be assigned to group A or group B by your teacher.

1. Prepare your set-ups as shown below.

Group A
cold water
hot water

Group B
hot water
cold water

2. Measure the temperature of the water in your beaker and basin. Record the measurements in the table provided on the next page.

Containers	Temperature (°C)			
	Start of experiment		End of experiment	
	Group A	Group B	Group A	Group B
Basin				
Beaker				

3. Arrange your set-ups as shown on the right and measure the temperature of the water in your beaker after ten minutes. Record the measurements in the table given above.

4. How has the temperature of the water in the beakers changed for both groups?

    (a) Group A's experiment: _____

    (b) Group B's experiment: _____

5. How has the temperature of the water in the basins changed for both groups?

    spoon A   spoon B

    (a) Group A's experiment: _____

    (b) Group B's experiment: _____

6. Now, label two metal spoons as spoon A and spoon B. Touch them and note how they feel.

spoon A   spoon B

warm water   cold water

7. Place spoon A in a cup of warm water. Place spoon B in a cup of cold water. Remove the spoons after two minutes. Touch the spoons again.

(a) Does spoon A feel hotter or colder now? _____

(b) Explain how the heat flow between spoon A and the water caused this change in temperature.

_____

(c) Does spoon B feel hotter or colder now? _____

(d) Explain how the heat flow between spoon B and the water caused this change in temperature.

_____

Conclusion

Heat flows from _____ to _____ objects. When

something _____ heat, its temperature _____.

When something _____ heat, its temperature _____.

 My notes   Give some examples of things that happen due to heat gain and heat loss.

_____

_____

Activity 3.1 Expansion and contraction — solid

Aim: To observe the effects of heat gain and heat loss on solids

Materials needed: Metal ball and ring set, Bunsen burner

Procedure to carry out

Your teacher will carry out this experiment.

1. Place the ball through the ring.
   Can the ball go through the ring? _____

2. Heat the ball over the flame for two minutes. Then try to place the ball through the ring.

   (a) Can the ball go through the ring after it has been heated?

   _____

   (b) How has the ball changed?

   _____

   (c) Did the ball gain or lose heat when it was heated?

   _____

3.   Allow the ball to cool. Try to place the ball through the ring again.

(a)   Can the ball go through the ring this time?

_____

(b)   How has the ball changed?

_____

(c)   Did the ball gain or lose heat when it was cooled down?

_____

Process recess

Observing and inferring
When you form a possible explanation based on your observation, you are **inferring**.

Draw lines below to match what you observed to what you inferred for the above activity.

What I observed	What I inferred
At first, the metal ball could go through the ring.	The metal ball became smaller when it lost heat.
After it was heated, the metal ball could not go through the ring.	The metal ball is slightly smaller than the ring.
After it was cooled, the metal ball could go through the ring.	The metal ball became bigger when it gained heat.

Activity 3.2 Expansion and contraction — liquid and gas

Aim: To observe the effects of heat gain and heat loss on liquids and gases

Materials needed: Test tube, coloured water, rubber bung, glass tube, white board marker, pair of tongs, basin of hot water, balloon, thin glass bottle

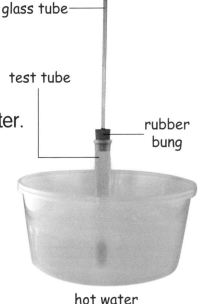

glass tube
test tube
rubber bung
hot water

Procedure to carry out

Your teacher will carry out this experiment.

1. Fill the test tube completely with coloured water.

2. Fit the rubber bung and glass tube to the test tube tightly.

3. Mark the water level in the glass tube with a white board marker.

4. Hold the test tube using a pair of tongs and place it in the basin of hot water.

   (a) What happened to the water level in the glass tube?

   _____

   (b) What caused this change?

   _____

5. Remove the test tube from the hot water.

(a) What happened to the water level in the glass tube?

_____

(b) What caused this change?

_____

6. Place a balloon over the mouth of a thin glass bottle.
Place the glass bottle in the basin of hot water.
Wait and observe what happens.

(a) What happened to the balloon?

_____

(b) What caused this change?

_____

_____

_____

My notes   How does heat loss or heat gain affect
liquids and gases?

_____

_____

_____

Activity 3.3 Changes in states of matter

Aim: To observe the change in state of a solid due to heat loss and heat gain

Materials needed: Ice cube, plate

Procedure to carry out

ice cube

1. Place an ice cube on a plate.
   Observe the ice cube for one minute.

   (a) What is happening to the ice cube?

   _____

   (b) Is the ice cube gaining or losing heat?

   _____

   (c) Draw arrows to show the direction in which heat is flowing.

ice cube

air in the surroundings

water

Activity 3.4 Heat flow

Aim: To find out how heat flows

Materials needed: Metal rod, three thumbtacks, candle, match, retort stand

Procedure to carry out

Your teacher will carry out this experiment.

1. Light a candle and drip some wax on the metal rod.
    Place a thumbtack on the wax before it hardens.
    Using the same method, place another two thumbtacks
    on the metal rod in the positions as shown below.

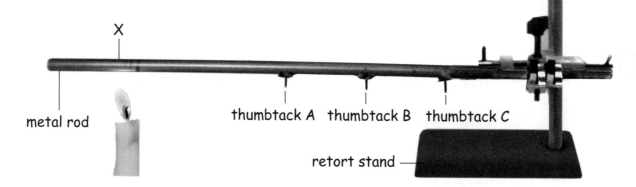

Predict what you will see if the rod was heated at position X
as shown above.

_____

_____

2. Use a retort stand to hold the metal rod at one end. Hold the metal rod over the lighted candle. Heat the rod at position X.

   (a) Is your prediction correct?

   _____

   (b) In which order did the thumbtacks drop off the metal rod?

   _____

   _____

   (c) Explain why the thumbtacks dropped off in this order.

   _____

   _____

   _____

   _____

   _____

   _____

Conclusion

If one object is hotter than the other, then heat will flow from the

_____ object to the _____ object.

Activity 3.5 Good and poor conductors

Aim: To find out which material is a better conductor of heat

Materials needed: Metal teaspoon, plastic teaspoon, styrofoam cup, hot water (about 90 °C), butter

Procedure to carry out

plastic teaspoon

butter

metal teaspoon

1. With the back of the teaspoons, scoop up a little butter. Try to ensure that the amount of butter on both teaspoons is the same.

2. Next, place the two teaspoons into a styrofoam cup that is filled with hot water.

3. Observe what happens to the butter and find out on which teaspoon the butter slides down first.

Conclusion

The butter on the _____ teaspoon slid down first. This shows that heat reached the butter on the _____ teaspoon first. Therefore, metal is a _____ conductor of heat and it allows heat to travel through it quickly. Plastic is a _____ conductor of heat and it does not allow heat to travel through it easily.

Activity 3.6 Keep it hot

Aim: To plan an experiment to find out which type of cup is best for keeping a drink warm

Materials needed: Styrofoam, metal and ceramic cups, thermometer, measuring cylinder, watch, basin of tap water, hot water (about 70 °C)

You may use the experiment planner that is provided below to plan your experiment.

ceramic cup

styrofoam cup

metal cup

Procedure to carry out

1. Pour the same amount of hot water into all three cups.

2. Use a thermometer to measure the temperature of the water in all the cups.

3. Record your results in the table on the next page.

4. Place all the cups in a basin of tap water.

5. After three minutes, measure the temperature of the water in the cups again and write it down in the table provided on the next page.

Experiment Planner

Variable to change: _____

Variables to keep the same:

_____

_____

_____

_____

Results

Types of cups used	Temperature of water in the beginning (°C)	Temperature of water at the end (°C)
Styrofoam		
Metal		
Ceramic		

Conclusion

Based on the above observation, the best type of cup for keeping drinks warm when it is placed in a basin of tap water is the

_____.

Explain why.

_____

BLANK

Published by Marshall Cavendish Education

An imprint of Marshall Cavendish International (Singapore) Private Limited

A member of Times Publishing Limited

Times Centre, 1 New Industrial Road, Singapore 536196

Customer Service Hotline: (65) 6411 0820

E-mail: tmesales@sg.marshallcavendish.com

Website: www.marshallcavendish.com/education/sg

First published 2001

Second edition 2008

Reprinted 2009, 2010

ISBN 978-981-01-8730-9

Edited by: Gerald Koh, Ivan Lee, Jayanthie Krishnan, Jessie Lau,
Linda Lee, Mark Lim, Usha M. Nathan, Yee Win May

Designed by: Cephas Chew, Goh Lizhen, Jamie Wong, Yuliana,
Joanalita Sulaiman Lai, Won Hwee Lay

Illustrated by: Anuar Abdul Rahim, Goh Soo Eng, Tay Bock Lan

Cover design by: Cephas Chew, Won Hwee Lay

Cover illustration by: Tay Bock Lan

Printed in Singapore by Times Printers, www.timesprinters.com

Acknowledgements

We are grateful to the following organisation and individuals:

- Models and their families
- Addest Technovation Pte Ltd: **P 5** (centre right)
- All those who have kindly loaned us items for the photos featured